The Best Greek

Recipe Book

The Tastiest Traditional Greek Recipes in
One Place

BY: Valeria Ray

License Notes

A Special Reward for Purchasing My Book!

Thank you, cherished reader, for purchasing my book and taking the time to read it. As a special reward for your decision, I would like to offer a gift of free and discounted books directly to your inbox. All you need to do is fill in the box below with your email address and name to start getting amazing offers in the comfort of your own home. You will never miss an offer because a reminder will be sent to you. Never miss a deal and get great deals without having to leave the house! Subscribe now and start saving!

https://valeria-ray.gr8.com

Contents

Traditional Greek Recipes

MMMMMMMMMMMMMMMMMMMMMMMMMMMMMM

(1) Greek Moussaka

This is the perfect meaty Greek casserole you can make whenever you want to impress your friends and family with your Greek cooking skills.

Serving Size: 8 servings

Cooking Time: 1 hour and 20 minutes

List of Ingredients:

- 2 pounds of ground beef
- 2 Tablespoons of extra virgin olive oil
- 1 onion, chopped
- 1 red bell pepper, stems removed and chopped
- 4 cloves of garlic, minced
- 1 teaspoon of allspice
- 1 teaspoon of powdered cinnamon
- 1 teaspoon of cayenne pepper
- ½ teaspoons of powdered ginger
- 1 teaspoon of black pepper
- 1 tablespoon of dried oregano
- 2 Tablespoons of tomato paste
- ½ cup of dried red wine
- 1 lemon, zest only
- 2 Tablespoons of lemon juice
- Dash of salt
- 1 stick of butter
- ½ cup of all-purpose flour
- 1 teaspoon of salt
- 4 cups of whole milk
- 4 egg yolks
- 1 bay leaf

- ½ teaspoons of powdered nutmeg
- 3 eggplants
- ½ cup of salt
- 8 cups of water
- 2 to 3 Yukon gold potatoes
- 1 cup of Pecorino Romano cheese, grated
- Extra virgin olive oil, as needed

MMMMMMMMMMMMMMMMMMMMMMMMMMMMM

Methods:

1. In a pot set over medium to high heat, fill with 8 cups of water and dash of salt. Slice the tops and bottoms off of the eggplants. Slice into rounds that are ¼ inch in size. Add into the pot. Set aside to rest for 15 to 20 minutes. Remove and drain on a plate lined with paper towels.

2. In a skillet set over medium to high heat, add in the ground beef. Cook for 8 to 10 minutes or until browned. Add in the chopped onions and chopped red bell pepper. Season with a dash of salt. Cook for an additional 5 minutes or until soft.

3. Add in the minced garlic, powdered cinnamon, ground allspice, cayenne pepper, powdered ginger, dash of black pepper, dried oregano and tomato paste. Stir well to mix. Cook for another 2 to 3 minutes.

4. Add in the dried red wine. Allow to come to a simmer. Lower the heat to low. Cook for 20 minutes. Turn off the heat of the stove. Add in the lemon zest and lemon juice. Season again with a dash of salt. Stir well to mix.

5. Peel the gold potatoes and slice into rounds that are ¼ inch in size. Place into a pot set over medium to high heat. Cover with salted water and allow to come to a boil. Cook for 6 to 8 minutes or until slightly soft. Drain and set aside.

6. Prepare the béchamel. In a pot set over medium heat, add in the milk. Allow to heat up until it reaches 160 degrees. Remove from heat.

7. In a separate pot set over medium heat, add in the butter. Once melted, add in the all-purpose flour. Whisk until smooth in consistency. Cook for 1 minute. Pour in the steamed milk, bay leaf, powdered nutmeg and dash of salt. Cook for 15 minutes over low heat until reduced. Toss out the bay leaf.

8. In a bowl, add in the egg yolks. Whisk until lightly beaten. Add in a ladle of the béchamel and whisk well to mix. Pour into the main béchamel sauce. Simmer over low heat.

9. Preheat the oven to 350 degrees.

10. In a casserole dish, add a layer of the potatoes, overlapping them slightly. Top off with the eggplant slices. Cover with the meat sauce. Add the remaining eggplant slices over the meat. Sprinkle half of the cheese over the zucchini slices. Ladle the béchamel over the top. Top off with the remaining cheese.

11. Place into the oven to bake for 35 to 45 minutes or until browned on the top.

12. Remove and set aside to cool for 15 minutes before serving.

(2) Greek Chicken and Potatoes

This is a simple and filling dish that you can make any night of the week. It is incredibly easy to make and hits the spot after a long day of work.

Serving Size: 4 to 5 servings

Cooking Time: 1 hour and 30 minutes

List of Ingredients:

- 1, 3 ½ pound chicken, whole
- 3 lemons
- 1/3 cup of extra virgin olive oil
- Dash of salt and black pepper
- 2 Tablespoons of dried oregano
- 11 cloves of garlic, minced
- 8 red potatoes, cut into quarters

MMMMMMMMMMMMMMMMMMMMMMMMMMMM

Methods:

1. Preheat the oven to 350 degrees. Place a sheet of parchment paper onto a baking sheet.

2. Place the chicken with the breast side facing down onto a flat surface. Slice the chicken in half along the back bone. Repeat on the breast side. Separate the chicken into two halves and place onto the baking sheet with the skin side facing up.

3. Squeeze fresh juice from the lemon onto the chicken halves. Pour half of the olive oil over the chicken. Season with a dash of salt and black pepper.

4. Sprinkle 1 tablespoon of the dried oregano and half of the minced garlic over the chicken. 5. Place the red potato quarters into a bowl. Add in the remaining olive oil, remaining minced garlic, dried oregano and juice from the second lemon over the top. Season with a dash of salt and black pepper. Toss well until coated.

5. Arrange the potatoes around the chicken.

6. Place into the oven to bake for 1 hour and 15 minutes or until the chicken is cooked through.

7. Remove and serve immediately.

(3) Greek Tortellini Salad

This is a tasty Greek salad dish that you can make whenever you are craving something on the lighter side. It is perfect to serve during your next potluck.

Serving Size: 8 servings

Cooking Time: 20 minutes

Ingredients for the salad:

- 1, 20 ounce pack of cheese tortellini
- 1 ½ cups of grape tomatoes, sliced into halves
- 1 cucumber, chopped
- 1 cup of kalamata olives, pits removed and chopped
- ½ of a red onion, chopped
- ¾ cup of feta cheese, crumbled
- Ingredients for the dressing:
- ¼ cup of extra virgin olive oil
- 3 Tablespoons of red wine vinegar
- 1 clove of garlic, minced
- ½ teaspoons of dried oregano
- Dash of salt and black pepper

MMMMMMMMMMMMMMMMMMMMMMMMMMMM

Methods:

1. In a pot set over medium to high heat, fill with salted water. Allow to come to a boil. Add in the cheese tortellini. Cook according to the directions on package. Drain and set aside.

2. Transfer the tortellini into a bowl. Add in the sliced grape tomatoes, chopped cucumber, chopped kalamata olives, chopped red onion and crumbled feta cheese. Stir gently to mix.

3. Prepare the dressing. In a separate bowl, add in the olive oil, red wine vinegar, minced garlic and dried oregano. Season with a dash of salt and black pepper. Pour over the top of the salad. Toss to coat.

4. Serve immediately.

(4) Roasted Greek Lemon and Garlic Potatoes

Make these delicious Greek style potatoes as a side dish to your next late-night Greek dinner meal. These potatoes are so delicious, you will want to make them as often as possible.

Serving Size: 4 to 6 servings

Cooking Time: 1 hour

List of Ingredients:

- 2 pounds of Yukon potatoes, sliced into wedges
- 4 cloves of garlic, minced
- ½ cup of extra virgin olive oil
- 1/3 cup of lemon juice
- 2 Tablespoons of mustard
- 1 tablespoon of dried oregano
- ½ Tablespoons of dried basil
- Dash of salt and black pepper

MMMMMMMMMMMMMMMMMMMMMMMMMMMMMM

Methods:

1. Preheat the oven to 400 degrees. Place a sheet of parchment paper onto a baking sheet.

2. In a bowl, add in the olive oil, minced garlic, lemon juice, mustard, dried oregano and dried basil. Season with a dash of salt and black pepper. Whisk until mixed.

3. Add in the Yukon potato wedges. Toss well until coated in the sauce.

4. Transfer the potatoes onto the baking sheet. Cover with a sheet of aluminum foil.

5. Place into the oven to bake for 50 minutes. Remove the foil. Continue to bake for an additional 10 minutes or until golden.

6. Remove from the oven. Allow to cool for 10 minutes before serving.

(5) Greek Zucchini and Feta Fritters

Make these delicious fritters as an early morning treat. One bite and I guarantee your friends and family will become hooked.

Serving Size: 4 servings

Cooking Time: 40 minutes

List of Ingredients:

- 2 pounds of zucchini
- 2 eggs, beaten
- ounces of feta cheese
- 4 Tablespoons of mint, chopped
- 4 Tablespoons of parsley, chopped
- ¾ cup of all-purpose flour
- 1 cup of extra virgin olive oil, for frying
- Dash of salt and black pepper

MMMMMMMMMMMMMMMMMMMMMMMMMMMMMM

Methods:

1. Slice the ends off of the zucchini. Grate the zucchini into a bowl and transfer into a colander. Season with 1 tablespoon of salt. Stir well to mix. Set aside to drain for 20 to 25 minutes. Squeeze the excess moisture out of the zucchini. Transfer into a bowl.

2. In the bowl, add in the eggs, chopped parsley, chopped dill, chopped mint and all-purpose flour. Season with a dash of black pepper. Stir gently to mix.

3. Add in the feta cheese and fold gently to incorporate.

4. In a skillet set over medium to high heat, add in the olive oil.

5. Shape the zucchini mix into patties. Place into the skillet. Cook for 5 minutes on each side or until golden. Transfer onto a plate lined with paper towels to drain.

6. Serve immediately.

(6) Greek Eggplant Dip

If you need a delicious homemade dip to serve during your next dinner party, then this is the perfect dip recipe for you to prepare.

Serving Size: 3 to 4 servings

Cooking Time: 1 hour and 30 minutes

List of Ingredients:

- 2 eggplants
- 4 cloves of garlic, peeled and minced
- ¼ cup of extra virgin olive oil, extra for serving
- 3 Tablespoons of lemon juice
- ¾ teaspoons of salt
- ¼ teaspoons of black pepper
- Parsley leaves, chopped and for garnish
- Kalamata olives, pits removed, sliced, for garnish

MMMMMMMMMMMMMMMMMMMMMMMMMMMM

Methods:

1. Preheat the oven to 400 degrees.

2. Place the eggplants onto a baking sheet lined with a sheet of aluminum foil. Prick over the surface with a fork. Place into the oven to bake for 1 hour or until soft. Remove and set aside to cool.

3. Peel the skin from the eggplant and slice in half. Scoop out the flesh and chop. Set into a colander. Set aside to drain for 15 minutes.

4. Transfer the eggplant flesh into a bowl. Mash with a fork.

5. Add in the minced garlic, extra virgin olive oil, lemon juice, and chopped parsley. Season with a dash of salt and black pepper. Stir well to mix.

6. Cover and set into the fridge to chill for 1 hour.

7. Serve with extra parsley, sliced olives and drizzle of olive oil over the top.

(7) Chicken Souvlaki

This is an authentic Greek recipe that is so easy to make, I know you are going to want to make it every chance you get.

Serving Size: 4 to 6 servings

Cooking Time: 20 minutes

List of Ingredients:

- 1 ½ pounds of chicken, boneless, skinless and cut into pieces
- 5 cloves of garlic, peeled and minced
- 2 Tablespoons of extra virgin olive oil
- 1 tablespoon of dried oregano
- Dash of salt and black pepper
- 1 lemon, juice only
- Baby arugula, for topping
- Red onions, sliced and for topping
- Pita breads
- Feta cheese, crumbled

MMMMMMMMMMMMMMMMMMMMMMMMMMMMM

Methods:

1. In a Ziploc bag, add in the chicken pieces, extra virgin olive oil, minced garlic, dried oregano, dash of salt and black pepper. Stir well to mix. Seal the bag and set into the fridge to chill for 30 minutes. 2. Thread the chicken onto metallic skewers.

2. Preheat an outdoor grill to medium or high heat. Place the chicken skewers onto the grill. Grill for 8 minutes or until cooked through. Transfer onto a plate and set aside.

3. Place the pita bread onto serving plates. Remove the chicken from the skewers and place onto the pita breads. Top off with the baby arugula, red onions and crumbled feta cheese.

4. Serve immediately.

(8) Greek Tomato and Feta Shrimp

This is an easy Greek style dish that you will love if you love the taste of shrimp. It is easy to make and makes for a quick and satisfying lunch or dinner.

Serving Size: 4 servings

Cooking Time: 50 minutes

List of Ingredients:

- 4 Tablespoons of extra virgin olive oil
- ¾ cup of shallots, chopped
- 4 cloves of garlic, chopped
- 1, 28 ounce can of tomatoes, chopped
- 1 ½ teaspoons of salt
- ¼ teaspoons of pepper
- 1 teaspoon of powdered cumin
- ½ teaspoons of crushed red pepper flakes
- 1 tablespoon of honey
- 1 ½ pounds of shrimp, peeled
- 6 ounces of feta cheese
- ¾ teaspoons of dried oregano
- 2 Tablespoons of mint, chopped

MMMMMMMMMMMMMMMMMMMMMMMMMMMMMM

Methods:

1. Preheat the oven to 400 degrees.

2. In a skillet set over low to medium heat, add in the olive oil. Add in the shallots and garlic. Cook for 5 to 8 minutes or until soft.

3. Add in the chopped tomatoes, crushed red pepper flakes, powdered cumin and honey. Season with a dash of salt and black pepper. Stir well to mix. Allow to come to a boil. Lower the heat to low. Cook for 15 to 20 minutes or until thick in consistency.

4. Remove from heat. Add in the shrimp Crumble the feta cheese over the top.

5. Sprinkle the oregano over the top.

6. Place into the oven to bake for 10 to 15 minutes or until the shrimp is pink in color or until cooked through.

7. Increase the temperature of the oven to a broil. Continue to bake for 1 to 2 minutes or until golden on the top.

8. Remove and allow to rest for 5 minutes.

9. Serve with a garnish of chopped mint.

(9)   Greek Quesadillas

If you love the flavor of homemade quesadillas, then this is the perfect dish for you to make. Topped off with a homemade tzatziki, this is a dish even the pickiest of eaters won't be able to resist.

Serving Size: 8 servings

Cooking Time: 30 minutes

List of Ingredients:

- 8, 8 inch flour tortillas
- 1, 10 ounce pack of spinach, chopped
- ½ cup of sun-dried tomatoes in olive oil, sliced julienne style
- ½ cup of kalamata olives, pits removed and chopped
- 1 cup of mozzarella cheese, shredded
- 1 cup of feta cheese, crumbled
- 1 tablespoon of dill, chopped

Ingredients for tzatziki sauce:

- 1 cup of plain Greek yogurt
- 1 English cucumber, chopped
- 2 cloves of garlic, pressed
- 1 tablespoon of dill, chopped
- 1 tablespoon of lemon juice
- 1 teaspoon of lemon zest
- 1 teaspoon of mint, chopped
- Dash of salt and black pepper
- 2 Tablespoons of extra virgin olive oil

MMMMMMMMMMMMMMMMMMMMMMMMMMMMM

Methods:

1. Prepare the tzatziki sauce. In a bowl, add in the Greek yogurt, chopped cucumber, pressed garlic, chopped dill, lemon juice, lemon zest and chopped mint. Season with a dash of salt and black pepper. Drizzle the olive oil over the top. Stir well to mix.

2. Cover and place into the fridge to chill for 10 minutes.

3. Preheat the oven to 400 degrees. Place a sheet of parchment paper onto a baking sheet.

4. Top off the flour tortillas with the spinach, tomatoes, chopped kalamata olives, shredded mozzarella cheese, chopped dill and crumbled feta cheese. Cover with another tortilla. Transfer onto the baking sheet.

5. Place into the oven to bake for 8 to 10 minutes.

6. Remove and serve immediately with the tzatziki sauce.

(10) Greek Meatballs

If you love the taste of meatballs, then this is the perfect meatball dish for you to make. It is made with a Greek flavor that is hard to resist.

Serving Size: 5 servings

Cooking Time: 35 minutes

Ingredients for the meatballs:

- 1 red onion, grated
- 1 pound of lean ground beef
- ounces of ground pork
- 2 cloves of garlic, minced
- 1 cup of panko breadcrumbs
- 1 egg
- ¼ cup of parsley, chopped
- 6 mint leaves, chopped
- ½ teaspoons of dried oregano
- 1 tablespoon of extra virgin olive oil
- ¾ teaspoons of salt
- Dash of black pepper

Ingredients for serving:

- ½ cup of all-purpose flour
- 3 Tablespoons of extra virgin olive oil
- Parsley, chopped
- Tzatziki sauce

MMMMMMMMMMMMMMMMMMMMMMMMMMMMMM

Methods:

1. Prepare the meatballs. In a bowl, add in the grated red onion, lean ground beef, ground pork, minced garlic, panko breadcrumbs, egg, chopped parsley, chopped mint leaves, dried oregano and olive oil. Season with a dash of salt and black pepper. Stir well to mix.

2. Shape the meat mix into 1 inch sized balls.

3. In a skillet set over medium to high heat, add in the remaining olive oil.

4. Dredge the meatballs in the all-purpose flour until coated on all sides. Add into the skillet. Cook for 5 minutes on all sides or until cooked through. Transfer onto a plate.

5. Serve with the chopped parsley and Tzatziki sauce.

(11) Greek Avocado Salad

If you love the taste of avocado, then this is definitely one salad recipe I know you won't be able to get enough of.

Serving Size: 4 servings

Cooking Time: 45 minutes

List of Ingredients:

- 2 chicken breasts, boneless, skinless and cut into halves
- Ingredients for the dressing:
- ¼ cup of extra virgin olive oil
- ¼ cup of lemon juice
- 1 tablespoon of red wine vinegar
- 2 teaspoons of garlic, minced
- 2 Tablespoons of dried oregano
- 1 teaspoon of salt
- Dash of black pepper

Ingredients for the salad:

- 4 cups of romaine lettuce, shredded
- 2 cucumbers, thinly sliced
- 2 tomatoes, cut into wedges
- ½ of a green bell pepper, seeds removed and thinly sliced
- ½ of a red onion, thinly sliced
- 7 ounces of feta cheese, cut into cubes
- ½ cup of kalamata olives, pits removed and cut into halves

- 1 avocado

MMMMMMMMMMMMMMMMMMMMMMMMMMMMMM

Methods:

1. Prepare the dressing. In a shallow dish, add in all of the ingredients for the dressing. Whisk well to mix. Set aside ½ cup of the dressing for serving.
2. Add the chicken breast halves into the remaining dressing. Stir well to coat.
3. Cover and set aside to marinate for 30 minutes.
4. Prepare the salad. In a bowl, add in all of the ingredients for the salad. Toss well to mix.
5. In a skillet set over medium to high heat, add in the marinated chicken. Cook for 5 to 10 minutes on each side or until cooked through. Remove and set aside to rest for 5 minutes before slicing. Transfer into the salad.
6. Drizzle the remaining dressing over the top.
7. Serve.

(12) Greek Gyros with Tzatziki

If there is one dish that is synonymous with authentic Greek cooking, it is gyros. This is a filling dish that you will want to make as often as possible.

Serving Size: 4 to 6 servings

Cooking Time: 30 minutes

List of Ingredients:

- 2 pounds of chicken thighs, boneless and skinless

Ingredients for the marinade:

- 3 cloves of garlic, minced
- 1 tablespoon of white wine vinegar
- 3 Tablespoons of lemon juice
- 1 tablespoon of extra virgin olive oil
- 3 Tablespoons of Greek yogurt
- 1 ½ Tablespoons of dried oregano
- 1 teaspoon of salt
- Dash of black pepper

Ingredients for the tzatziki:

- 2 cucumbers, grated
- 1 ¼ cups of plain Greek yogurt
- 1 tablespoon of lemon juice
- 1 tablespoon of extra virgin olive oil
- ½ clove of garlic, minced
- ½ teaspoons of salt
- Dash of black pepper
- Ingredients for the salad:
- 3 tomatoes, seeds removed and chopped
- 3 cucumbers, chopped
- ½ of a red onion, peeled and chopped
- ¼ cup of parsley leaves, chopped
- Dash of salt and black pepper

Ingredients for serving:

- 4 to 6 pita breads

MMMMMMMMMMMMMMMMMMMMMMMMMMMMM

Methods:

1. Prepare the marinade. Add all of the ingredients for the marinade into a Ziploc bag. Stir gently to mix. Add in the chicken. Seal the bag. Place into the fridge to chill for 2 hours to marinate.

2. Prepare the tzatziki. In a bowl, add in the grated cucumber. Add in the Greek yogurt, lemon juice, olive oil and minced garlic. Season with a dash of salt and black pepper. Toss well to mix. Set aside to rest for 20 minutes.

3. Prepare the salad. In a bowl, add in the chopped tomatoes, chopped cucumbers, chopped red onion and chopped parsley leaves. Season with a dash of salt and black pepper. Toss well to mix.

4. Prepare an outdoor grill to medium or high heat. Grease the grates of the grill with cooking spray. Place the chicken onto the grill. Grill for 4 to 5 minutes or until cooked through. Remove and set aside to rest for 5 minutes.

5. Remove the meat from the chicken and shred finely. Place onto the pita breads. Top off with the salad and a drizzle of tzatziki over the top.

6. Roll up and serve.

(13) Greek Stuffed Red Bell Peppers

This is a delicious and savory appetizer you can make to serve to your family during your next Greek inspired feast.

Serving Size: 6 servings

Cooking Time: 10 minutes

List of Ingredients:

- 6 red bell peppers, roasted
- 1 cup of feta cheese, crumbled
- ¼ cup of plain Greek yogurt
- 2 Tablespoons of parsley, chopped
- ¼ teaspoons of salt
- 2 cloves of garlic, mashed
- 2 Tablespoons of lemon juice
- 1 tablespoon of extra virgin olive oil

MMMMMMMMMMMMMMMMMMMMMMMMMMMM

Methods:

1. In a bowl, add in the crumbled feta cheese and plain Greek yogurt. Stir well until smooth in consistency.
2. Stuff the roasted red bell peppers with this mix.
3. In a separate bowl, add in the lemon juice and extra virgin olive oil. Stir well to mix. Drizzle over the top of the red bell peppers.
4. Serve immediately.

(14) Greek Seven Layer Dip

This is the perfect dip recipe for you to serve during your next dinner party. It is so delicious, your guests will be begging you for the recipe.

Serving Size: 6 servings

Cooking Time: 15 minutes

List of Ingredients:

- 1, 15.5 ounce can of garbanzo beans, drained with liquid reserved
- 2 ½ Tablespoons of tahini
- 2 Tablespoons of lemon juice
- 2 cloves of garlic, minced
- ½ teaspoons of powdered cumin
- ½ teaspoons of salt
- 2 Tablespoons of extra virgin olive oil
- 1 1/3 cups of plain Greek yogurt
- 1 ½ Tablespoons of parsley, chopped
- 1 tablespoon of dill, minced
- 1 cup of English cucumber, chopped
- 1 cup of grape tomatoes, chopped
- 1/3 cup of black olives, thinly sliced
- ½ cup of feta cheese, crumbled
- 3 Tablespoons of red onion, chopped

MMMMMMMMMMMMMMMMMMMMMMMMMMMMMM

Methods:

1. In a food processor, add in the garbanzo beans, tahini, lemon juice, 1 clove of minced garlic, powdered cumin and dash of salt. Pulse for 1 minute. Slowly add in the olive oil and 2 tablespoons of the juice from the garbanzo beans. Continue to pulse until smooth in consistency.

2. Spread the hummus into a baking dish.

3. In a bowl, add in the plain Greek yogurt, chopped parsley, minced dill and remaining clove of garlic. Stir well to mix. Drop in dollops over the hummus in the baking dish.

4. Top off with the chopped cucumber, chopped grape tomatoes, sliced black olives and chopped red onion. Sprinkle the crumbled feta cheese over the top.

5. Cover and set into the fridge to chill until ready to serve.

(15) Greek Spanakopita

If you have never tried traditional Spanakopita, then this is one Greek dish that you will love. It is perfect to make whenever you want to impress your friends and family with something special.

Serving Size: 12 servings

Cooking Time: 25 minutes

Ingredients for the filling:

- 16 ounces of spinach, chopped
- 2 bunches of flat leaf parsley, chopped
- 1 yellow onion, chopped
- 2 cloves of garlic, minced
- 2 Tablespoons of extra virgin olive oil
- 4 eggs
- 10.5 ounces of feta cheese, crumbled
- 2 teaspoons of dried dill weed
- Dash of black pepper

Ingredients for the crust:

- 1, 16 ounce pack of phyllo dough, thawed
- 1 cup of extra virgin olive oil

MMMMMMMMMMMMMMMMMMMMMMMMMMMM

Methods:

1. Preheat the oven to 325 degrees.
2. Prepare the filling. In a bowl, add in the chopped spinach, chopped parsley, chopped yellow onion, minced garlic, olive oil, eggs, crumbled feta cheese, dried dill weed and dash of black pepper. Stir well to mix.
3. Unroll the phyllo dough on a flat surface.
4. Grease a baking dish and add two sheets of phyllo dough into the dish. Brush the top with extra virgin olive oil. Add two more sheets and brush again with olive oil. Repeat with 2/3 of the phyllo dough. Pour the filling over the top. Top off with two sheets of phyllo dough. Brush the top with olive oil. Repeat with the remaining phyllo dough.
5. Place into the oven to bake for 1 hour or until golden.
6. Remove and cool for 10 minutes. Slice into squares and serve.

(16) Greek Lemon Chicken Skewers

These delicious chicken skewers are perfect to make during your next family barbecue. Made with a fresh tzatziki sauce, this is a dish everybody will love.

Serving Size: 4 servings

Cooking Time: 3 hours and 10 minutes

List of Ingredients:

- 1 ½ pounds of chicken breasts, cut into cubes
- 3 Tablespoons of lemon juice
- 1 tablespoon of red wine vinegar
- 1 tablespoon of extra virgin olive oil
- 2 cloves of garlic, minced
- 2 teaspoons of dried oregano
- ½ teaspoons of dried parsley
- ½ teaspoons of coriander
- ¾ teaspoons of salt
- Dash of black pepper

Ingredients for the tzatziki sauce:

- 1 cup of English cucumber, peeled and chopped
- 1 ½ cups of plain Greek yogurt
- ½ of a lemon, juice only
- 1 tablespoon of dill, chopped
- 1 teaspoon of grated garlic
- ½ teaspoons of salt
- Dash of black pepper

MMMMMMMMMMMMMMMMMMMMMMMMMMMMM

Methods:

1. Prepare the chicken. In a bowl, add in the chicken breast cubes, lemon juice, red wine vinegar, olive oil, minced garlic, dried oregano, dried parsley and coriander. Season with a dash of salt and black pepper. Stir well to mix.

2. Cover and set into the fridge to marinate for 3 hours.

3. Preheat an outdoor grill to medium or high heat. Grease the grates of the grill with cooking spray.

4. Thread the marinated chicken onto metallic skewers. Place onto the grill. Cook for 3 to 4 minutes on each side or until cooked through. Remove and set aside to rest.

5. Prepare the sauce. In a bowl, add in the chopped cucumber, plain Greek yogurt, lemon juice, chopped dill and grated garlic. Season with a dash of salt and black pepper. Stir gently to mix.

6. Serve the chicken with the tzatziki sauce.

(17) Greek Lemon Soup

If you need a dish to help you feel better whenever you are feeling under the weather, then look no further!

Serving Size: 4 servings

Cooking Time: 25 minutes

List of Ingredients:

- 1 tablespoon of extra virgin olive oil
- 1 onion, chopped
- 6 cups of chicken broth
- ½ cup of arborio rice
- 3 eggs, beaten
- 2 cups of chicken, cooked
- 2 lemons, juice and zest only
- 2 Tablespoons of white miso paste
- Dash of salt

MMMMMMMMMMMMMMMMMMMMMMMMMMMMM

Methods:

1. In a saucepan set over medium to high heat, add in the olive oil and chopped onions. Cook for 5 minutes or until soft.
2. Add in the chicken broth and arborio rice. Allow to come to a boil. Lower the heat to low. Cook for 15 to 20 minutes or until soft.
3. Add in the chicken broth and eggs. Whisk until lightly beaten.
4. Add in the cooked chicken, lemon juice and lemon zest. Stir gently to mix. Continue to cook for 5 minutes.
5. Remove from heat. Season with a dash of salt.
6. Serve immediately.

(18) Greek Chicken and Lemon Rice

This is a simple and delicious Greek dish that is perfect to prepare during those busy weeknights. It is so simple to make, all you need is one pot to put it together.

Serving Size: 5 servings

Cooking Time: 1 hour

Ingredients for the chicken and marinade:

- 5 chicken thighs, skin-on and bone-in
- 1 to 2 lemons, zest only and 4 Tablespoons used for lemon juice
- 1 tablespoon of dried oregano
- 4 cloves of garlic, minced
- ½ teaspoons of salt

Ingredients for the rice:

- 1 ½ Tablespoons of extra virgin olive oil, separated
- 1 onion, chopped
- 1 cup of long-grain rice
- 1 ½ cups of chicken broth
- ¾ cup of water
- 1 tablespoon of dried oregano
- ¾ teaspoons of salt
- Dash of black pepper
- Ingredients for the garnish:
- Parsley, chopped
- Lemon zest

MMMMMMMMMMMMMMMMMMMMMMMMMMMM

Methods:

1. Prepare the chicken and marinade. In a Ziploc bag, add in the chicken thighs, lemon zest, lemon juice, dried oregano, minced garlic and dash of salt. Seal the bag and stir well to mix. Set aside to marinate for 20 minutes.

2. Preheat the oven to 350 degrees.

3. In a skillet set over medium to high heat, add in ½ tablespoons of the olive oil. Add in the marinated chicken with the skin side facing down. Cook for 5 to 8 minutes or until browned. Flip and continue to cook for an additional 8 minutes. Remove and set aside.

4. Drain the grease from the skillet. Add in 1 tablespoon of olive oil. Add in the chopped onion. Cook for 5 minutes or until soft. Add in the rice, chicken broth, water, dried oregano and marinade. Season with a dash of salt and black pepper. Stir well to mix. Allow to simmer for 30 seconds.

5. Place the chicken over the top.

6. Cover and set into the oven to bake for 35 minutes. Remove the cover. Continue to bake for an additional 10 minutes or until the rice is soft.

7. Remove and allow to rest for 10 minutes.

8. Serve with a garnish of chopped parsley and lemon zest.

(19) Greek Macaroni Pie

This is a Greek style dish you can make to spoil your friends and family. It is made with minced lamb and gooey mac and cheese to make the ultimate dinner dish.

Serving Size: 6 servings

Cooking Time: 1 hour

List of Ingredients:

- 1 cup of elbow macaroni
- 2 Tablespoons of extra virgin olive oil
- 1 onion, chopped
- 2 cloves of garlic, minced
- 2 pounds of minced lamb
- 1 cup of pasta water
- ¾ of a lamb stock cube
- 2 teaspoons of pureed tomato
- 1 teaspoon of cumin seeds, toasted and ground
- 1 teaspoon of powder cinnamon
- 1 tablespoon of mint, chopped
- 2 Tablespoons of butter
- 2 Tablespoons of all-purpose flour
- ½ cup of plain Greek yogurt
- ½ cup of whole milk
- ½ cup of grated cheddar cheese, evenly divided
- Dash of sea salt and black pepper

MMMMMMMMMMMMMMMMMMMMMMMMMMMMMM

Methods:

1. Preheat the oven to 375 degrees.

2. In a pot set over medium to high heat, fill with salted water. Allow to come to a boil. Add in the elbow macaroni. Cook for 8 to 10 minutes or until soft. Drain and set the macaroni aside. Reserve 1 cup of the water.

3. In a saucepan set over medium to high heat, add in the olive oil. Add in the chopped onion and minced garlic. Cook for 8 to 10 minutes or until soft.

4. Add in the minced lamb. Season with a dash of salt and black pepper. Cook for 8 to 10 minutes or until browned.

5. Add in the lamb stock cube and reserved pasta water. Add in the powdered cinnamon, pureed tomato, ground cumin seeds and chopped mint. Stir gently to mix. Allow to simmer for 10 to 15 minutes or until thick in consistency.

6. In a separate saucepan set over medium heat, add in the butter. Once melted, add in the all-purpose flour. Whisk until smooth in consistency. Cook for 1 minute. Remove from heat. Add in the whole milk and Greek yogurt. Stir well to incorporate. Set back over medium heat. Add in half of the grated cheddar cheese. Cook for 2 minutes or until smooth in consistency.

7. Add in the cooked elbow macaroni. Stir well to mix. Transfer into a greased baking dish. 8. Spoon the lamb over the top. Add the remaining macaroni. Sprinkle the remaining grated cheddar cheese over the top.

8. Place into the oven to bake for 30 minutes or until golden.

9. Remove and serve immediately.

(20) Greek Orzo Salad

This is the perfect salad dish to make right in time for spring time. It is a delicious and filling Greek flavored salad you can make any night of the week.

Serving Size: 6 servings

Cooking Time: 20 minutes

Ingredients for the salad:

- 1 cup of dried orzo pasta
- 1 cucumber, chopped
- 2 tomatoes, chopped
- 1 red onion, chopped
- ½ cup of kalamata olives, pits removed and chopped
- ¼ cup of parsley, chopped
- ½ cup of feta cheese, crumbled

Ingredients for the dressing:

- ¼ cup of extra virgin olive oil
- ¼ cup of red wine vinegar
- 1 tablespoon of lemon juice
- 1 teaspoon of honey
- ½ teaspoons of powdered garlic
- ½ teaspoons of black pepper
- 1 teaspoon of salt

MMMMMMMMMMMMMMMMMMMMMMMMMMMMMM

Methods:

1. Prepare the orzo pasta according to the directions on the package. Drain and set aside.

2. Prepare the dressing. In a bowl, add in the olive oil, red wine vinegar, lemon juice, honey and powdered garlic. Season with a dash of salt and black pepper. Whisk until smooth in consistency.

3. Prepare the salad. In a bowl, add in the cooked orzo pasta, chopped cucumber, chopped tomatoes, chopped red onion, chopped kalamata olives and chopped parsley. Pour the dressing over the top. Toss until coated.

4. Sprinkle the crumbled feta cheese over the top.

5. Serve immediately.

(21) Homemade Greek Pita Bread

With the help of this delicious recipe, you won't have to purchase store-bought pita bread ever again. Make this pita bread whenever you are craving Greek cuisine.

Serving Size: 8 servings

Cooking Time: 2 hours and 5 minutes

List of Ingredients:

- 2 cups of all-purpose flour
- ½ cup of whole wheat flour
- 2 teaspoons of salt
- 2 teaspoons of instant yeast
- 1 cup of warm water
- 1 tablespoon of extra virgin olive oil

MMMMMMMMMMMMMMMMMMMMMMMMMMMMM

Methods:

1. In a bowl, add in the all-purpose flour, whole wheat flour, dash of salt, instant yeast, warm water and olive oil. Stir well until mixed.

2. Cover and set the dough aside to rest for 1 hour and 30 minutes.

3. Preheat the oven to 475 degrees.

4. Divide the dough into 8 pieces. Shape each piece in a ball. Cover and set aside to rest for 10 minutes.

5. Roll each dough ball into a disc that is 4 inches in size. Allow to rest for 10 minutes. Roll again into a 7 to 8 inch circle. Brush the discs with water. Place onto a greased baking sheet. 6. Place into the oven to bake for 2 to 3 minutes. Remove and place into a skillet set over medium to high heat. Continue to cook for 1 minute or until browned on both sides.

6. Remove and rest for 10 minutes before serving.

(22) Greek Cream Cheese Lemon Coffee Cake

This is a great tasting Greek dish you can make whenever you have a strong sweet tooth that needs to be satisfied. One bite and you will become hooked.

 Serving Size: 16 servings

Cooking Time: 50 minutes

Ingredients for the cream cheese;

- 8 ounces of Greek cream cheese, soft
- ¼ cup of white sugar
- 1 egg
- 1 ½ teaspoons of lemon juice

Ingredients for the coffee cake:

- 1 ½ cups of all-purpose flour
- ½ teaspoons of baker's style baking powder
- ¼ teaspoons of baker's style baking soda
- ¼ teaspoons of salt
- ½ cup of vegetable oil
- ¾ cup of white sugar
- 1 egg
- ½ cup of Greek yogurt
- 1 lemon, zest only
- 1 tablespoon of lemon juice

Ingredients for the crumb topping:

- ½ cup of all-purpose flour
- ¼ cup of white sugar
- 2 Tablespoons of butter, cold and cut into cubes
- Powdered sugar, for dusting

Methods:

- Preheat the oven to 350 degrees. Add a sheet of parchment paper into a baking dish.
- Prepare the cream cheese layer. In a bowl, add in the cream cheese, white sugar, egg and lemon juice. Whisk until smooth in consistency.
- Prepare the coffee cake. In a separate bowl, add in the all-purpose flour, dash of salt, baking powder and soda. Stir well to mix. Add in the Greek yogurt, lemon zest and lemon juice. Stir well until creamy in consistency.
- Pour into the baking dish. Spread the cream cheese mix over the top.
- Prepare the crumb topping. In a bowl, add in the all-purpose flour, white sugar and cold butter pieces. Stir well until crumbly in consistency. Sprinkle over the top of the cream cheese layer.
- Place into the oven to bake for 40 to 45 minutes.
- Remove and dust with the powdered sugar.
- Slice into squares and serve.

(23) Greek Doughnuts

These are the perfect doughnuts to make whenever you are craving something on the sweet side. Make these for those picky eaters in your home.

Serving Size: 4 servings

Cooking Time: 15 minutes

List of Ingredients:

- 7 ounces of all-purpose flour
- 1.7 ounces of cornstarch
- 1 ½ teaspoons of dry yeast
- Dash of salt
- 1 tablespoon of honey
- 10 ounces of warm water
- Vegetable oil, for frying

MMMMMMMMMMMMMMMMMMMMMMMMMMMMM

Methods:

1. In a bowl, add in the all-purpose flour, cornstarch, dry yeast, dash of salt, honey and warm water. Stir well until just mix.
2. Set aside to rest for 30 minutes.
3. In a pot, add in 3 inches of vegetable oil. Heat until the oil reaches a temperature of 350 degrees.
4. Divide the dough into 1 inch sized balls. Drop into the hot oil. Fry for 5 minutes or until golden. Drain and repeat.
5. Serve with a drizzle of honey.

(24) Greek Rice Pudding

This is one of the most authentic Greek recipes that you can make today. It is so tasty, this Greek dish will soon become a dessert of choice.

Serving Size: 2 servings

Cooking Time: 25 minutes

List of Ingredients:

- 1 ½ cups of whole milk
- 2 cups of water
- 1 cup of white rice
- ¾ cup of white sugar
- 1 tablespoon of pure vanilla
- 2 eggs
- 1 to 2 teaspoons of powdered cinnamon, for topping

MMMMMMMMMMMMMMMMMMMMMMMMMMMMM

Methods:

1. In a saucepan set over medium to high heat, add in the water and white rice. Allow to come to a boil. Lower the heat to low. Cook for 20 minutes or until the rice is cooked through.

2. In a bowl, add in the white sugar, pure vanilla and eggs. Whisk until smooth in consistency. Set this mix aside.

3. In the rice, add in the whole milk. Continue to cook for 5 minutes or until thick in consistency. Add in the sugar mix and stir well until evenly blended.

4. Pour into serving bowls and allow to cool completely.

5. Serve with a sprinkle of powdered cinnamon over the top.

(25) Greek Lemon and Butter Cookies

These cookies are a classic holiday sweet that is served throughout the holiday season. They are incredibly easy to make and will satisfy all who try it.

Serving Size: 36 servings

Cooking Time: 50 minutes

List of Ingredients:

- 2 cups of all-purpose flour
- 1 cup of almond flour
- ½ teaspoons of baker's style baking powder
- ¼ teaspoons of sea salt
- 2 sticks of butter, soft
- 1 cup of powdered sugar
- 2 cups of powdered sugar, for rolling
- 1 egg yolk
- ¼ cup of lemon juice
- 1 tablespoon of lemon zest

MMMMMMMMMMMMMMMMMMMMMMMMMMMMM

Methods:

1. Preheat the oven to 350 degrees. Place two sheets of parchment paper onto two baking sheets.

2. In a bowl, add in the all-purpose flour, almond flour, dash of salt and baking powder. Stir well to mix.

3. In a separate bowl, add in the butter and 1 cup of powdered sugar. Beat with an electric mixer until smooth in consistency. Add in the egg yolks, lemon juice and lemon zest. Continue to beat for 2 minutes or until fluffy in consistency.

4. Add in the flour mix. Continue to beat until just mixed.

5. Transfer the dough onto a flat surface. Knead for 1 minute or until smooth. Roll the dough into balls that are 1 inch in size. Transfer onto the baking sheets.

6. Place into the oven to bake for 18 to 20 minutes or until golden. Remove and set aside to rest for 5 to 10 minutes.

7. In a bowl, add in the remaining 2 cups of powdered sugar. Roll the cookies in the powdered sugar and set aside to cool completely.

8. Serve.

About the Author

A native of Indianapolis, Indiana, Valeria Ray found her passion for cooking while she was studying English Literature at Oakland City University. She decided to try a cooking course with her friends and the experience changed her forever. She enrolled at the Art Institute of Indiana which offered extensive courses in the culinary Arts. Once Ray dipped her toe in the cooking world, she never looked back.

When Valeria graduated, she worked in French restaurants in the Indianapolis area until she became the head chef at one of the 5-star establishments in the area. Valeria's attention to taste and visual detail caught the eye of a local business person who expressed an interest in publishing her recipes. Valeria began her secondary career authoring cookbooks and e-books which she tackled with as much talent and gusto as her first career. Her passion for food leaps off the page of her books which have colourful anecdotes and stunning pictures of dishes she has prepared herself.

Valeria Ray lives in Indianapolis with her husband of 15 years, Tom, her daughter, Isobel and their loveable Golden Retriever, Goldy. Valeria enjoys cooking special dishes in her large, comfortable kitchen where the family gets involved in preparing meals. This successful, dynamic chef is an inspiration to culinary students and novice cooks everywhere.

●●●●●●●●●●●●●●●●●●●●●●

Author's Afterthoughts

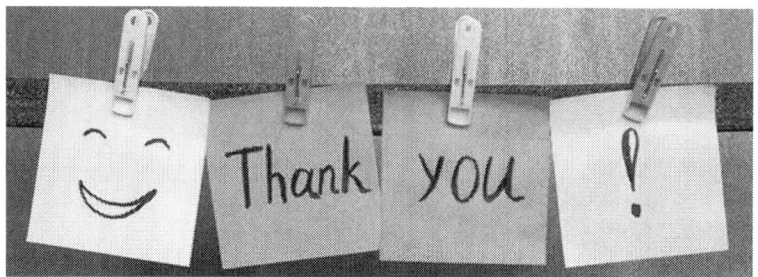

Thank you for Purchasing my book and taking the time to read it from front to back. I am always grateful when a reader chooses my work and I hope you enjoyed it!

With the vast selection available online, I am touched that you chose to be purchasing my work and take valuable time out of your life to read it. My hope is that you feel you made the right decision.

I very much would like to know what you thought of the book. Please take the time to write an honest and informative review on Amazon.com. Your experience and opinions will be of great benefit to me and those readers looking to make an informed choice.

With much thanks,

Valeria Ray

Printed in Poland
by Amazon Fulfillment
Poland Sp. z o.o., Wrocław

51221906R00052